to my

x x

ARRAN & AYRSHIRE

NESS PUBLISHING

2   Turnberry Lighthouse, built in 1873, stands on the South Ayrshire coast near the site of Turnberry Castle, where Robert the Bruce was born in 1274.

ARRAN & AYRSHIRE

The dome-shaped island of Ailsa Craig can be seen on the right. Turnberry is internationally famed for its three championship golf courses.

Welcome to Ayrshire!

In one sense Ayrshire is just like the rest of Scotland – it has everything! On the other hand, what is found within its boundaries is a unique collection of sights and experiences. Ayrshire contains extremes in Scotland's landscapes: the mountainous Isle of Arran is one of the country's best-loved places to enjoy a holiday, while within its mainland districts are areas of industry, fertile farmland, a long coastline and historical curiosities of many kinds. Being located on Scotland's south-west coast gives the region a generally mild climate that allows the growth of palm trees and gave rise to many resorts once the era of holidays for the masses arrived. Coastal towns like Largs, Millport (on the Isle of Cumbrae) and indeed Ayr itself are examples of this phenomenon and still have much to offer to summer visitors.

The territory covered in this book relates to Ayrshire as it existed until 1975. The local government re-organisation of that year saw Ayrshire absorbed into Strathclyde Region. As part of that process, Arran was transferred from Bute to Cunninghame, the northernmost of the four district councils that administered the 'Ayrshire' part of Strathclyde. With further re-organisation in 1996, regions and districts disappeared, being replaced by 32 unitary council areas. Thus what had started out as the traditional county of Ayrshire is today divided between North Ayrshire, East Ayrshire and South Ayrshire. The only major difference in their coverage compared with

4

Setting off for Arran: the ferry *Caledonian Isles* sails from Ardrossan, with the island stretching out invitingly along the horizon.

the 'old' Ayrshire is that North Ayrshire (the former Cunninghame, approximately) retains the Isle of Arran. Arran is therefore included, having been part of 'Ayrshire' territories since 1975.

Returning to features historical, the most notable of the ancient sites are found on Arran, the west coast of which has a wealth of stone circles, chambered cairns and standing stones. These go back as much as 4,500 years, begun in Neolithic times and gaining the stones that remain today during the Bronze Age. The greatest concentration is at Machrie Moor, a sacred landscape where a complex story of belief and ritual has unfolded over thousands of years. The most impressive of the Machrie stones can be seen in this book's cover picture. The one shown opposite gives an idea of the scale of the larger stones, which stand up to 5.5m/18ft tall. Although this one appears to be solitary, it was once part of a circle, the other stones of which have been removed or lie buried in the peat that now covers the moor.

But it is in the realm of Scotland's literary legacy that Ayrshire has its greatest claim to fame, in the person of

6   Standing stone at Machrie Moor 3, one of a network of fascinating ritual sites at this location.

Robert Burns. Scotland's Bard was born in Alloway (just south of Ayr) on 25th January 1759 and spent much of his life in Ayrshire. Alloway is 'Mecca' for Burns' devotees and the principal points of pilgrimage are illustrated. One of those is Poet's Walk, where various Burns' characters can be seen, such as the giant-size mouse pictured opposite. Poet's Walk connects Burns' Birthplace to the superb new Robert Burns Birthplace Museum where the bard's life is shown through a new lens at this state-of-the-art exhibition.

This book begins its journey with an exploration of Arran, then island-hops to Great Cumbrae before reaching the mainland at Largs in North Ayrshire. Our mostly coastal route through North Ayrshire is followed by a circuit of East Ayrshire that takes in the beautiful hill country around Loch Doon. Finally, we meander southwards through South Ayrshire, finishing not far from neighbouring Galloway. If Ayrshire has not yet reached your radar as a must-see place to visit, prepare to be surprised!

'Wee, sleekit, cowrin, tim'rous beastie' at Poet's Walk, Alloway.   7

8   Arrival in Brodick by ferry gives this enticing view of one of Arran's principal villages and its lovely setting – as first impressions go, this takes some beating.

Part of Arran's appeal is that it is large enough to give visitors (and residents for that matter) plenty to explore, while being compact enough to engender a feeling of familiarity with the whole island.

10 From the air, Arran's proximity to Ayrshire can be appreciated. The ferry crossing takes under an hour. Clearly this is a winter view, with the Arran mountains dressed to impress in their winter clothes

Hill walkers are spoilt for choice on Arran, as is apparent in this view from the ferry. Beinn Nuis **11** (792m/2597ft) rises steeply above Glen Rosa. Arran's top 10 peaks are all above 2000ft (610m).

12 Even as one disembarks from the ferry the sight of Goatfell, Arran's highest mountain at 874m/2866ft, draws the eye.

The Isle of Arran Heritage Museum is a 'must' as there is no better way to get a stimulating overview of the island's story. Meet 5,000-year-old Clachaig man and investigate a Bronze Age grave.

14 With its oldest part dating back to the 13th century, Brodick Castle is a good example of how what began as a fortress has evolved into a country house as conditions and circumstances have allowed.

Part of the formal gardens at Brodick Castle, giving an idea of the view over Brodick Bay. The Castle, Garden and Country Park offer a wonderful combination of heritage, nature, walks and relaxation. 15

16 Brodick Castle was granted to James, Lord Hamilton, by James IV, together with the title Earl of Arran, and remained in Hamilton hands until 1958 when it was taken into the care of the National Trust for Scotland.

Perhaps the most impressive walking route into the Arran mountains is via Glen Rosa. Here, on a day **17** of mixed conditions, there is sun on Glenrosa Water while craggy Cir Mhor lurks in cloud.

18 Now we embark on a clockwise circular tour of Arran on which the first stop is Lamlash. Pictured is a memorial to the hundreds who were removed from Arran during the clearance years of 1829-1840.

The appeal of Lamlash can be appreciated in this view across its sheltered bay. It is the island's largest **19** village and architecturally most attractive settlement thanks to numerous elegant Victorian buildings.

20 A little further south at Whiting Bay are the impressive Glenashdale Falls. Left, both main cascades are captured sharp while on the right the upper falls are seen with long-exposure blur.

Whiting Bay offers a good view of Holy Island which can be accessed by boat trips from Lamlash **21** and has some good walks, including the 314m/1030ft summit of Mullach Mor.

22 From the southern tip of Arran near Kildonan, a sunrise view across to the island of Pladda, with its lighthouse just visible.

The village of Blackwaterfoot on the south-west coast shows off its 'bijou' harbour, with waterfall in **23** full flow neatly framed in the arch of the bridge, all in all a delightful scene.

24 A panorama taken from the eastern side of the Kintyre peninsula, looking across Kilbrannan Sound at Arran's western side. These days, this is by far the less developed side of the island, but going

back to Neolithic and Bronze Age times it was a hive of activity. Many sites remain, offering tantalising hints about life then, while at the same time keeping many secrets.

26 Machrie Moor is the epicentre of ancient activity, where a network of sites speaks of huge effort over many centuries. These two stones are part of Moss Farm Road cairn/circle and are passed on the way to . . .

. . . Fingal's Cauldron (Machrie Moor 5), a complex double circle with 25 boulders visible but evidence **27** of more in former times. The stones in the cover picture (MM2) can just be made out in the distance.

28 A mile or so to the north, the stones at Auchagallon form a circle; however it is not clear whether they are a stone circle as such, or the kerb stones of a cairn. A cist (stone coffin) was found here in the 1800s.

Seabirds are of course abundant in Arran. Left: the attention of all bar one of these Cormorants has just **29** been gained by something out to sea. Right: a Black Guillemot lowers its feet prior to splashdown.

30 Moving on to the northern tip of Arran, Lochranza Castle guards the bay. The ruins are of 16th-century origin, but replaced an earlier 13th-century structure that is said to have been visited by Robert the Bruce.

The Isle of Arran Distillery is the only one on the island and began production in 1995. **31**
Its whisky has already won awards. It has a Visitor Centre and offers tours of the distillery.

32 Now heading south through north-east Arran, the route cuts through the edge of the mountains. This is North Glen Sannox burn, near the beginning of one of the paths to the mountains.

The Arran mountains provide plenty of scrambling opportunities, as shown by these **33** pinnacles on the ridge above Glen Sannox.

34 Seal appeal! These common seals basking on the rocks near Sannox village make an endearing sight. Although seal numbers around Scotland in general are falling, there seem to be plenty in Arran.

The charming coastal village of Corrie boasts two harbours. At the northerly one, Corrie Port, **35** a replica Viking Longboat makes a surprising sight. Inset: figurehead on the longboat.

36 With our circuit of Arran almost complete, we'll finish on a high note. The dramatic summit of Cir Mhor (798m/2618ft) is seen in much better conditions than previously (p.17), viewed from Caisteal Abhail.

This is the reverse view, from Cir Mhor's tiny summit looking back to Caisteal Abhail **37** (859m/2818ft). Linking ridges make it possible to climb both these peaks in one expedition.

38 Ayrshire's next biggest island is Great Cumbrae. The resort town of Millport stretches around the island's southern bay. Its growth took off from 1833 when the building of a pier enabled Clyde steamers to call.

Millport's most intriguing attraction is the tiny but beautifully formed Cathedral of the Isles, which **39** began as a theological college in 1851. The church itself seats only 50 or so worshippers. See also p.80.

40 North Ayrshire overlooks the mouth of the Clyde estuary and hillside viewpoints, like this one on the Kelburn Estate near Largs, provide grand panoramic views. From left to right are the islands of

Great Cumbrae with Bute behind, then the Cowal Peninsula across in Argyll and finally the seaside 41
town of Largs at the foot of the hills (its name comes from the Gaelic for hillside).

42 A closer view of Largs reveals the ferry shuttling off on its frequent crossing to Cumbrae. Largs is both a resort and a retirement town – a pleasant place to visit and in which to live.

This picture shows Largs doing its best impression of a more Mediterranean location, **43** complete with palm trees. The Isle of Cumbrae is in the distance.

44 In a town of much Victorian architecture, this striking Art Deco gem of a building is hard to miss. Originally opened in 1935, Nardini's is synonymous with a trip 'doon the water'.

Vikingar is a major attraction in Largs, which recreates the days of Norse influence and tells the **45** story of the Battle of Largs in 1263. This exhibit gives an idea of home life in that era.

46 A castle like no other! This colourful make-over creates an entirely different impression of the 1581-built castle, centrepiece of the Kelburn Castle, Country Centre & Estate, located just south of Largs.

Continuing southwards, Saltcoats has a fine beach which attracts many day-trippers from Glasgow and
Ayrshire itself. The name Saltcoats comes from the early industry of making salt by evaporating sea water.

48   In neighbouring Stevenston, the beach is captured on a day when temperatures must have been very low to freeze the edge of the sea. Arran's snowy mountains can be seen in the distance.

Left: A few miles inland, Kilwinning's Abbey was once one of Scotland's most impressive. **49**
Right: returning to the coast at Irvine, a trawler heads for port on a chilly day.

50 Now we turn our attention to East Ayrshire, starting in Kilmarnock. The town centres on Kilmarnock Cross, seen here, with a statue of Robert Burns and his printer John Wilson on the right.

The Dick Institute, funded by Kilmarnock-born James Dick, opened in 1901 **51** and houses the town's Library, Museum and Art Gallery.

52 Dean Castle, Kilmarnock, goes back to the 14th century. Thoroughly restored in the 20th century, today it makes a fine sight and houses many historic artefacts. It is surrounded by parkland.

Left: a young fallow deer stag in Dean Castle Park. Right: travelling east from Kilmarnock, **53** we come to the town of Newmilns where this fine Towerhouse is a classic example of its type.

54 Continuing east, Darvel is our next calling point. Left: Hastings Square, with its enigmatic stone ball atop its pillar. Right: bust of Alexander Fleming, discoverer of penicillin, who was born near Darvel.

A picture of tranquillity now, but in May 1307 Robert the Bruce and some 600 men defeated an army **55** of up to 3,000 English here at Loudoun Hill. From this moment, support for him grew across Scotland.

56 The southern part of East Ayrshire is where the land begins to rise towards the hills that form the boundary with Dumfries and Galloway. And this is where Ayrshire takes on a more Highland look,

with beautiful Loch Doon enfolded in the surrounding hills into which it stretches for about five miles. Ruined Loch Doon Castle is situated near the head of the loch on its western shore.

58 Moving on to the town of Cumnock, something quite new is to be found in Old Cumnock Old Church. This beautiful mosaic, installed in 1966, illustrates the story of Jesus walking on the water.

Commissioned by the 5th Earl of Dumfries, Dumfries House near Auchinleck was designed by Robert **59** Adam and built from 1754 to 1759. What makes it unique is its exceptional range of original furniture.

60 Back on the Burns' trail, this is the Burns' House Museum in the town of Mauchline, where Burns lived and worked from 1784 to 1788. It is also where he met and married his great love Jean Armour.

Poosie Nansie ran this tavern in Mauchline which Burns frequented. The revelry of its clientele 61 of beggars and 'gangrel bodies' inspired *The Jolly Beggars*.

62 North-west of Mauchline is Dundonald Castle, built by Robert Stewart, probably to mark his accession to the throne as King Robert II in 1371. This huge structure is the third castle to have been built here.

And so to Ayr itself, an ancient and historic town that takes its name from the River Ayr seen here. **63**
The 'Auld Brig' of 1470 makes an interesting comparison with the 'new' bridge of 1878 beyond it.

64 Ayr's Auld Kirk is tucked away between the High Street and the river, accessed via Kirk Port.
A place of tranquillity from which to escape the busyness of the town.

Ayr has a wealth of fine structures from various eras, of which the County Building, **65** completed in 1822, is one.

66 The village of Alloway is only a couple of miles south of Ayr and, as noted in the introduction, is the heart of Burns' country. Robert Burns was born in this cottage in 1759 and died in Dumfries in 1796.

INSPIRED BY
SUPERSTITION
AND SONG

One of the beautifully preserved rooms in the cottage, which was built by William Burnes, **67**
Robert's father, in 1757. The family lived here for the first seven years of Robert's life.

SACRED
TO THE MEMORY OF
William Burns
FARMER in LOCHLIE,
who died on the 13th Feb 1784,
in the 63d year of his age.
AND OF
Agnes Brown
HIS SPOUSE
who died on the 14th Jan 1820,
in the 88 year of her age.

68 Left: Alloway Auld Kirk is famous as one of the settings in Burns' most famous poem *Tam O' Shanter*. Right: Burns' father William is buried here, with the headstone also commemorating his mother.

The Burns Monument stands in the Memorial Gardens close to the River Doon. In the style of a Grecian **69** Temple and 70ft high, it was designed by Sir Thomas Hamilton and erected from 1820 to 1823.

70 The Brig o' Doon is another key element in any Burns pilgrimage as it also features in *Tam O' Shanter*, when Tam flees across the bridge on horseback to escape from the pursuing witches.

Heading south from Alloway, not far from Maybole is Blairquhan. One of the finest Regency castles **71** in Scotland, it replaced an earlier 14th-century castle and was constructed from 1821 to 1826.

72 South-west of Maybole we come to the substantial remains of Crossraguel Abbey. It was founded in the mid 13th century as a Cluniac monastery. This view is from the top of the gatehouse.

This is Crossraguel's Towerhouse, built about 1530 as a fine residence for the Abbot. It replaced the earlier Abbot's house, some remnants of which can be seen in the background on the right. **73**

74 Culzean is undoubtedly one of Scotland's finest castles. It has developed via a well-trodden path from functional fortification, the recorded history of which goes back to the 1400s. As conditions allowed,

it grew into more of a home than a fortress, culminating in its 18th-century transformation into the neoclassical mansion seen opposite. Above: Fountain Court and the North Range.

76 There are several gardens at Culzean, all of which provide an ideal place to simply sit and enjoy the scene.

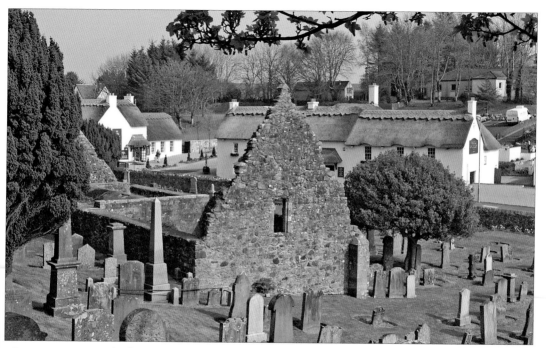

Continuing our southerly progress, this is the old churchyard in Kirkoswald. Robert Burns stayed in the village in 1775 and later based the two principal characters in *Tam o' Shanter* on local residents. **77**

78 The port of Girvan lies in the Carrick district of South Ayrshire. Its harbour remains busy, partly because it is the embarkation point for trips to Ailsa Craig (see p.2-3).

And finally, from Bennane Head a gorgeous seascape looking south towards Ballantrae. **79**
From here it is no great distance to Galloway, but that is another journey . . .

Published 2012 by Ness Publishing, 47 Academy Street, Elgin, Moray, IV30 1LR
Phone 01343 549663   www.nesspublishing.co.uk

All photographs © Colin Nutt except pp.2-3, 22, 36, 37, 48, 49 (both) & 79 © Keith Fergus;
p.10 © Guthrie Aerial Photography; p.65 © www.undiscoveredscotland.co.uk

Text © Colin Nutt
ISBN 978-1-906549-18-3

Front cover: Machrie Moor standing stones; p.1: statues of Tam o' Shanter and Souter Johnnie at
Souter Johnnie's Cottage, Kirkoswald; p.4: street sculpture in Kilmarnock; this page: detail from *The Adoration of the Lamb*
in the Cathedral of the Isles; back cover: Loch Doon

For a list of websites and phone numbers please turn over >

Websites and phone numbers (where available) for principal places featured in this book in order of appearance:

Machrie Moor stone circles: www.historic-scotland.gov.uk
Souter Johnnie's Cottage: www.nts.org.uk (T) 0844 493 2147
Caledonian MacBrayne: www.calmac.co.uk (T) 0800 066 5000
Isle of Arran: www.visitarran.net & www.visitarran.com
Robert Burns Birthplace Museum: www.nts.org.uk (T) 0844 493 2100
Brodick: www.brodick.org.uk
The Isle of Arran Heritage Museum: www.arranmuseum.co.uk (T) 01770 302636
Brodick Castle: www.nts.org.uk (T) 0844 493 2146
Auchagallon stone circle: www.historic-scotland.gov.uk
Lochranza Castle: www.historic-scotland.gov.uk
Isle of Arran Distillery: www.arranwhisky.com (T) 01770 830264
Isle of Cumbrae: millport.org
Cathedral of the Isles: www.cumbraecathedralfriends.com (T) 01475 530353
Kelburn Castle & Country Centre: www.kelburnestate.com (T) 01475 568685
Largs: www.largsonline.co.uk
Nardini's: www.nardinis.co.uk (T) 01475 675000
Vikingar: www.kaleisure.com (T) 01475 689777
Saltcoats: www.visitsaltcoats.com
Kilwinning Abbey: www.historic-scotland.gov.uk
Kilmarnock: www.kilmarnock.org.uk
Dean Castle: www.deancastle.com (T) 01563 522702
Loudoun Hill: www.loudounhillinn.com (T) 01560 320275
Old Cumnock Old Church: www.sacredscotland.org.uk